Anonymous

Rural Resorts and Summer Retreats Along the Line of the

Cumberland Valley Railroad

Including picnic parks and pleasure places

Anonymous

Rural Resorts and Summer Retreats Along the Line of the Cumberland Valley Railroad
Including picnic parks and pleasure places

ISBN/EAN: 9783337419547

Printed in Europe, USA, Canada, Australia, Japan

Cover: Foto ©Andreas Hilbeck / pixelio.de

More available books at **www.hansebooks.com**

RURAL RESORTS AND SUMMER RETREATS

ALONG THE LINE OF THE

CUMBERLAND VALLEY

Rustic Fountain in Mont Alto Park.

RAILROAD;

INCLUDING

Picnic Parks and Pleasure Places.

1881

INTRODUCTION.

The Valley.

NEARLY half a century has elapsed since the Cumberland Valley Railroad Company first broke ground for its pioneer enterprise in railroading, and laid the first rail of its line beyond the western shore of the Susquehanna river, upon a survey entering and hiding itself in the bosom of one of the richest and sweetest valleys that the sun of heaven shines upon; rich in the minerals of its mountains, and their pleasure nooks, and summer retreats; the fruits of its fields; the beauties of its scenery, and in the store of its traditional and historical lore; sweet with its healthful breezes which make music in its rustling grain fields and grow heavy with the breath of its flowers—a region where, when summer falls,

"It seems always afternoon."

In the shadow of its mountains, spread out like a panorama are views which combine all the elements of rural beauty unadorned, verging into the improvements of a modest civilization. Fields lie there, in fertility and in fairness equal to any within the confines of the Middle or Western States, through the emerald breadth of which wind in sinuous course, like threads of molten silver, two principal streams with their numerous tributaries, which civilization permits still to bear the names that the Indian gave them, as if to appease the still unexorcised spirit of his wrongs.

(3)

The names of Conococheague and Conodogwinit are landmarks in a history, the origin of which it is now claimed ante-dates the landing of Penn, the apostle of civilization on the shores of the Delaware, the bi-centennial of whose arrival is now at hand.

Peeping from these slopes of velvet green and silvered border are the homes of farmers, and, like pictures, rise before the vision towns and villages whose spires and belfries mark equi-distant points in a line of beauty stretching from where a silver gleam of waters marks the presence of the Susquehanna to a point where the whole is lost in the dimness of that hazy distance in which the parallel lines of mountain seem to meet and blend their blueness. And the glimmering track of the Cumberland Valley Railroad, like the great artery as it is of the busy life with which this scene is instinct, winds in gentle curve from village to village, and town to town, in the original line of civilization, marked first by the Indian moccasin, followed by the pack-horse hoof and wagon track; opening up this beautiful valley to the outside world, inviting the care-worn and heat-wearied denizen of the city to a delightful ride over a model road-bed, in new coaches perfectly equipped, to a brief sojourn in a region where the far past and the present are so closely blended that the very breezes whisper legends, and where the beauties of the country and the conveniences of the town pay tribute to each other.

THE RAILROAD.

Rudely-constructed railways were in use in Pennsylvania as early as 1812, around quarries and mines, but the first legislation in America authorizing a company to make a railroad for public use was the act of the Legislature of Pennsylvania of 31st of March, 1823, granting permission to Mr. Stevens, and others, to make a railway from Philadelphia to the Susquehanna at Columbia, a distance of eighty-four and one-half miles. This company, however, never prosecuted the work of constructing the road, but a railway was subsequently, in 1828, built by the State over the same route, at which time also the first survey for a similar road was made through the region of the Cumberland Valley, under the auspices of the State authorities.

The Cumberland Valley Railroad Company was incorporated on the 2d of April, 1831. A survey of the proposed route was at once instituted by W. Milnor Roberts, who had been chosen chief engineer of the new company. Mr. Roberts made his report to the board of directors of which Hon. Thomas G. McCulloh was president, on the 23d of October, 1835. This report showed that the whole length of the route as traced from the Susquehanna by way of Mechanicsburg, Carlisle, *Irwin's Mill*, Shippensburg, and *Thompson's Mill*, was forty-nine and one-eighth miles, about the same length as the turnpike then in operation, and six miles shorter than the route surveyed by order of the State in 1828. The maximum grade was thirty feet to the mile. The curves were few in number, all having radii exceeding half a mile.

In August, 1837, the first division of the Cumberland Valley Railroad, from Carlisle to within one and one-half miles of Harrisburg, was completed, and the first train of cars passed over the line on the twelfth of that month. The second division, extending from Carlise to Chambersburg, was opened on the 23d of November, 1837. In 1843 the Franklin Railroad, which extended from Chambersburg to Hagerstown, Maryland, indicated its intention of discontinuing business. This would have been a serious blow to the Cumberland Valley Railroad, as the Franklin was its connecting link with the National Turnpike Road at Hagerstown. The Cumberland Valley Railroad accordingly accepted a proposition from the Franklin to run their road for one-half the profits, after payment of expenses and repairs. The two roads were finally absolutely consolidated in 1865, two years after the destruction of the track of the Franklin by the Confederate army.

Closing his report of the date of January, 1843, president Watts says:—"If this country should ever again be blessed with the same amount of prosperity which we had a few years ago, and there is no reason why it should not, I do not hesitate to say that the stock of the Cumberland Valley Railroad will be profitable to its owners." How like a prophecy do these words sound when read in connection with a knowledge of the present condition of the Cumberland Valley Railroad, and with the thought of the mighty developments in which it must bear no insignificant part in the near future. By the recent completion of the Shenandoah Valley Railroad to Waynesboro, Virginia, the Cumberland Valley has become the trunk line of the system of railroads west and south of the Susquehanna, and its connecting link with the eastern and northern system which centres at Harrisburg. A through route has thus now been opened from all points west and east to the White Sulphur Springs in Virginia, thence, by other connecting links to be added in the near future, to New Orleans and the far South.

MAIN LINE.

THE BRIDGE

At Harrisburg, 104 miles from Philadelphia.

THIS structure which spans the Susquehanna river and forms the railroad connecting link between its eastern and western shores at this point is one of the most imposing of its kind in the State. It was built in 1839, destroyed by fire in 1844, and rebuilt immediately in its present compact shape. Its simple design and beautiful situation never fail of rendering it an object of interest to the stranger. It crosses the Susquehanna at one of its most interesting points. Along the eastern shore of the river as far as the eye can reach are visible the signs of a busy activity. To the left verging close to the water's edge lies the Capital city with its palatial residences, shaded streets and avenues. Centrally situated and most conspicuous is the mosque-like dome of the Capitol building, surrounded by the spires of many churches; hard by, the obelisk Monument in honor of the dead soldiers of the late war rears its head only to be outdone in its lofty aspirations by the "Stand Pipe" of the city water works, which rises like a slender light-house by the river's side. Across the river, nigh at hand, leading from the principal street of the city, runs the old foot and wagon bridge constructed in 1817. To the right along the shore disappearing in the distance extends that famous system of Iron Works, headed by "Paxton" and "Lochiel," and including the Pennsylvania Steel Works, marking their industry by a pillar of cloud by day and of fire by night, the lurid brightness of which blends with the moonlight on the river like the flashes of the aurora of the North with the summer twilight. Gazing upon the scene which the day

(7)

9

discloses here it is hard to believe that scarcely a century
and a half ago all that city was a howling wilderness with
no habitation of civilized being, save one, to break the
monotony of the river's wild border; but so it was, and
there in that little enclosure plainly visible on your left as
you leave the eastern shore to cross the bridge lies buried
the builder and owner of that habitation, John Harris, the
pioneer settler of this region. Though enclosed with iron
fence, no stately monument marks his grave, and no token,
save only the broken, decayed, and tottering trunk of a
once noble tree that was bearing blossoms when Penn landed,
and is preserved now only because it once served as the
stake to which unfriendly Indians bound and would have
burned save for timely aid, the living body of the brave
settler who now sleeps at its base. The story is as familiar
as a twice-told tale, we will not repeat it.

Skirting the western shore, broken only by the entrance
to the valley, where the bridge terminates, are the hills of
"Mother Cumberland" dotted, in the olden time, by the
wigwams of Indian villages, but green now with the
promise of the valley harvest. Nestling at the base of these
hills, to the right is the village of Fairview, and away to
the left, just visible in the mist which marks the spot
where the Susquehanna drinks up the waters of the Yellow
Breeches are the spires of New Cumberland; and between
the city with its industries upon the one hand, and the
country with its villages upon the other, sweeps in all its
grandeur the noble Susquehanna from a rift in the Kitta-
tinny mountains to the northward, onward through the
mountains of the south to the Chesapeake.

BRIDGEPORT.

1 mile from Harrisburg; 105 from Philadelphia.

WESTERN terminus of the bridge; consists of five or six
dwellings, a warehouse, and railroad enginehouse. At
this point the Northern Central Railway from Baltimore,

Md., to Canandaigua, N. Y. intersects the Cumberland Valley Railroad. Fort Washington, built for the protection of Harrisburg during the late war, lies on the height west of Bridgeport. The railroad has a double track from this point to Mechanicsburg.

WHITEHILL.

3 miles from Harrisburg; 107 from Philadelphia.

POST village in East Pennsboro; named after Hon. Robert Whitehill, who purchased the land from the Proprietaries in 1770. It is a part of the ancient manor of Louther and is a village of ten or twelve dwellings and a warehouse.

SHIREMANSTOWN.

5 miles from Harrisburg; 109 from Philadelphia.

A POST village, partly in Hampden and partly in Allen townships; settled in 1813; named after Daniel Shireman. It is now one of the neatest little villages in the valley in one of the coolest and most healthy spots, within twenty minutes ride of Harrisburg. Just the place for a business man in the city to rest with his family.
Population between 400 and 500.

MECHANICSBURG.

8 miles from Harrisburg; 112 from Philadelphia.

THE first town of the valley on the line of the railroad; incorporated as a borough, April 12th, 1828. The advantages of this town as a summer resting place are many. Less than half an hour's ride by rail from Harrisburg it is still far enough removed from the river to be entirely free of malarial influences. The town, which contains upwards of 3000 inhabitants, is noted for its culture and refinement, and the country around, which is accessible by well improved roads, is densely settled by a wealthy and industrious population. Gas and water companies supply the town with those necessary elements of comfort and convenience. Besides its common school system, Mechanicsburg has the advantage of two private institutions of learning, "The Cumberland Valley Institute" and "Irving Female College"; the last mentioned is a handsome and commodious building situated in the eastern end of the town in the midst of grounds beautifully laid out and thickly shaded by tall trees.

Mechanicsburg has seven churches and five hotels.

DILLSBURG JUNCTION.

9 miles from Harrisburg; 113 from Philadelphia.

AT this point the Cumberland Valley Railroad connects with the branch leading to Dillsburg and William's Grove, the famous picnic grounds, a description of which is given elsewhere.

KINGSTON.

12 miles from Harrisburg; 116 from Philadelphia.

A PRETTY little village in Silver Spring township, originally settled by Joseph Junkin, a Revolutionary soldier, but laid out by John King, after whom it is named, nearly sixty years ago. It is not only a pretty, but an exceedingly healthy spot, well supplied with water which is conducted in pipes from a never-failing spring.

MIDDLESEX STATION.

14 miles from Harrisburg; 118 from Philadelphia.

THIS station derives its name from the village of the same name picturesquely situated about a mile from railroad, at the confluence of Le Tort Springs with the Conodogwinit Creek in North Middleton Township. Middlesex was a point on the first "Indian track" to go westward in ancient times.

12

The Conodogwinit was crossed at this point and the track then ran by way of Sterrett's Gap, Concord, Burnt Cabins, &c., to the west of the Alleghenies. It was at Middlesex that Henry Dunning, an artificer of the Revolution, manufactured the first wrought cannon used in America.

SOUTH MOUNTAIN JUNCTION.

18 miles from Harrisburg; 122 from Philadelphia.

HERE, within the borough limits of Carlisle, the Cumberland Valley Railroad connects with the South Mountain Railroad leading to Mt. Holly Springs and Pine Grove Park, descriptions of which are elsewhere given.

CARLISLE.

19 miles from Harrisburg; 123 from Philadelphia.

THE history of no town in America is more worthy of extended mention than that of Carlisle. From the earliest times this place has been prominent. It has figured in all the eras of Pennsylvania's history, from the hour when the first hardy pioneer of civilization placed his foot upon its soil, to the present time. Romantic tales of border life, and thrilling adventure with the Indians, spring into life at mention of its name. Some of the most interesting episodes of the Revolutionary period were enacted within its borders, and it was the home of many who won for themselves fame in that early struggle for our liberties, and who now rest after their faithful labors in the hallowed precints of its ancient burial ground. Ephraim Blaine, John Armstrong, William Hendricks, George Stevenson, William Thompson, William Irvine, Robert Magaw, Frederick Watts, James McLean, and John Bannister Gibson, are a few of that bright galaxy of heroes and statesmen whose names—for their military and civil services—will live in equal honor with the name of their birth-place or domicile through all time.

Carlisle is the county-seat of Cumberland county, and is called after the English town of the same name. It was founded in 1751 by the Proprietaries, who reserved for themselves desirable lands within its limits. It is handsomely laid out, the principal streets crossing each other at right angles. The square in the centre of the town, through which the railroad passes, is noticeable for the two ancient churches erected on the plots to the right, and the court house and market house to the left. One of these churches, the stone one with a tower, on the right of the railroad, the Presbyterian, has a history which antedates the

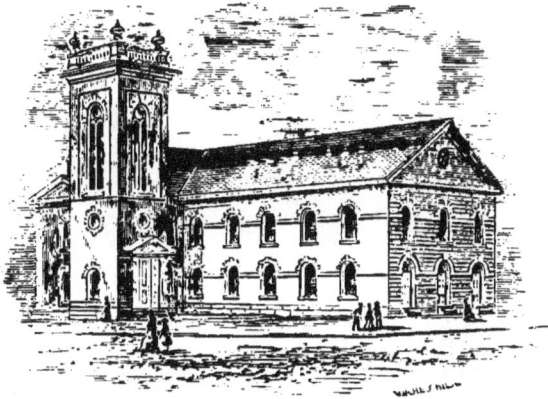

THE OLD PRESBYTERIAN CHURCH.

revolution. Dickinson College, named in honor of John Dickinson, President of the Supreme Executive Council of Pennsylvania, is situated in the western part of the town, also in view of the railroad. This ancient institution was incorporated by the legislature in 1783, and numbers many noted names amongst its alumni. A little to the east of the town, opposite South Mountain Junction, is the site of the extensive barracks erected, during the Revolutionary war by the labor of the Hessian prisoners captured at the battle of Trenton in 1776, for the accommodation of troops and the preservation of public stores. The original

DICKINSON COLLEGE.

barracks buildings were almost totally destroyed by Confederate troops in 1863, but the guard house and the walls of some of the buildings yet remain, specimens of the handiwork of the Hessian prisoners. The barracks having been rebuilt are now transformed into a Government Indian school, under the charge of Capt. R. H. Pratt, where young Indians, numbering over two hundred, are taught the arts of peace upon the very spot where their savage ancestors once figured in scenes of blood and carnage. The school is a Government experiment, which seems likely to prove successful. A visit to the place is full of interest.

In the late war Carlisle had also a part to play. The town was visited and occupied by a portion of Gen. Lee's army, on the eve of the battle of Gettysburg, under the command of Gens. Ewell and Jenkins. In departing from the town the Confederates became engaged in a skirmish with the Federal troops and the militia, who were approaching the place, during the prevalence of which a considerable number of shells and other warlike missiles were thrown into the town by the Confederates, which luckily did but little injury to property, though one Federal soldier was killed and fifteen wounded. Vestiges of this little affray are still pointed out to the stranger passing through Carlisle. A number of houses show marks of shells which are plainly visible from the railroad.

There are a number of natural curiosities near Carlisle. North of the town is Hogshead Spring, in a conical excavation nearly sixty feet in circumference. Some distance below the summit is an arched opening into a passage. At the bottom of this cavity is a pool of delicious water, cool and refreshing though apparently stagnant, for there are no visible means by which the basin receives or discharges it.

On the banks of the Conodogwinit, about a mile and a half from town, there is a somewhat noted cave. The entrance is by a semi-circular archway seven or more feet in height. So true and finished is the curve of this portal that the spectator is induced to believe that it has been perfected by art. The cavern is worth a visit, and, although dark and damp, will repay an examination by torch-light. Tradition has it that the Indians formerly made this place a deposit for their spoils and an asylum in seasons of danger. The population of Carlisle is about 6700.

GREASON and KERRSVILLE are flag-stations between Carlisle and Newville. Each is the nucleus of a future village, being at present prominent grain and produce depots.

NEWVILLE.

30 miles from Harrisburg; 134 from Philadelphia.
(9 miles by stage to Doubling Gap Springs.)

A HEALTHFUL and thriving town half a mile from the railroad station. Newville is deservedly a popular place of resort in the summer. It was incorporated February 26th, 1817. Through its borders flows the " Big Spring," a stream noted for its fine trout, which yearly attract thither merry disciples of Walton from all parts of the country. Within nine miles of Newville are the famous Doubling Gap Springs, with their healing waters, situated in the bosom of mountains, the weird surroundings and wild beauties of which gives zest to the legend which clings to them of that " Sandy Flash" of the Cumberland Valley, the once famous highwayman Lewis. From the plains this place appears high in the mountain, but when we get there we seem in a valley. There is a steep mountain before us, a steep mountain behind us, and at the head of the gap is another mountain. There is only one approach to the level fields below; all else is precipitous, steep, and in many places inaccessible. There are various points which may be visited hereabout. A grand view of the entire Cumberland Valley lies before the gazer from " Flat Rock" near the peak. For variety, beauty and picturesque effect the landscape can scarcely be exceeded by any in the country. At the Springs, which are white sulphur and chalybeate, a hotel is erected, where visitors are accommodated through the summer at reasonable rates. All the conveniences of a well-regulated summer resort are at hand.

Big Spring Hotel, at Newville station, is also thrown open to boarders during the summer, and is headquarters for the sportsmen who come to enjoy the fishing. Newville has about 1000 inhabitants.

OAKVILLE AND CAMP-GROUND.

34 miles from Harrisburg; 138 from Philadelphia.

THE little village of Oakville has of late days come into prominence, from the fact that it is the point nearest the commodious grounds of the " Carlisle District Camp Meeting Association" of the Methodist Episcopal Church, which lie adjacent to it. These grounds, which, with their buildings, are well arranged for the purpose, besides the religious use for which they are set apart, are frequently the objective point of pic-nic and other similar gatherings from all sections of the valley

SHIPPENSBURG.

41 miles from Harrisburg ; 145 from Philadelphia.

THE oldest town in the Cumberland Valley is Shippensburg. The incidents in its early history are replete with thrilling interest. During the French and Indian wars two forts were erected here, Fort Morris, in 1755, and Fort Franklin, in 1756. In 1755 it was the magazine for the stores of Braddock's army, being a principal point and place of rendezvous upon the old pack-horse line and later wagon route that led by the "Three-Mountain-Road" to Fort Pitt and the West. Shippensburg was the first seat of justice of Cumberland county, but enjoyed this honor for a short period only, the courts being removed to Carlisle at an early date. The settlement was incorporated into a borough in 1817 and still remains a place of prominence.

The enterprise of its inhabitants secured for it in 1871 the location there of the State Normal School of the seventh district. This is an imposing building situated upon an eminence at the eastern end of the town, and is one of the

NORMAL SCHOOL.

principal attractions of the place. The town is surrounded by beautiful drives; roads leading from it in all directions to neighboring towns, and the mountains which are in close proximity to it on either hand. The population is about 3000.

SCOTLAND.

47 miles from Harrisburg; 151 from Philadelphia.

THIS ancient settlement, formerly known as "Thompson's Mill," is situated in a delightful spot on the banks of the Conococheague creek, which is here spanned by a railroad bridge. This bridge was destroyed by Confederate troops under General Jenkins in June, 1863. The temporary structure then erected has since given place to a substantial one of iron. Picnics find ample accommodations in the neighborhood of Scotland and the Conococheague here is noted for its many fishing places. Scotland is the first station on the railroad in Franklin county. It contains two churches, Covenanters and United Brethren; three stores, a grist and saw mill, and planing mill. It has a population of about 250.

MONT ALTO JUNCTION.

48 miles from Harrisburg; 152 from Philadelphia.

AT this point the Cumberland Valley Railroad connects
with the Mont Alto Railroad leading to Waynesboro and
Mont Alto Park, of which mention is made elsewhere.

CHAMBERSBURG.

52 miles from Harrisburg; 156 from Philadelphia.

CHAMBERSBURG, the seat of justice of Franklin county
and the largest town in the valley, was founded in 1764,
by Benjamin Chambers, whose name it bears. It was
originally called Conococheague and Chambers' settlement.
During the French and Indian wars of 1755, the Revolution and intermediate wars, "Chambers' settlement" was a
small frontier village, almost the outpost of civilization.
A considerable trade was carried on with the most remote
settlements on the Pittsburg road by means of pack horses,
and, as a consequence the old town of Chambersburg grew
rapidly in trade and in population. During the late
war, Chambersburg was on several occasions visited by
raiding parties from the Southern army, and its deliberate
sacking and burning by the forces of McCausland on the
30th of July, 1864, is one of the darkest stains upon the
pages of the record of the late Rebellion. General Lee's
entire army passed through the town on his advance to the
ill-fated field of Gettysburg. The railroad crosses Market
street along which the the greater portion of the Southern
army marched. Several vestiges of the burning in 1864 are
still visible in various parts of the town.

The public buildings of Chambersburg are numerous and
present an attractive appearence, as do its private residences
which are nearly all new. The Court House is an imposing structure; the cupola contains a handsome clock with
illuminated dials, and is surmounted with a statue of

Benjamin Franklin, after whom the county is named. The Chambersburg Academy buildings are situated on an eminence commanding a view of the surrounding country. The first charter of this school was obtained from the State, in 1797, and the institution has been in existence ever since. Wilson Female College is situated a short distance north of Chambersburg. It is one of the most promising institutions in the country. It was handsomely endowed by its founder, and is rapidly acquiring a reputation of which its friends may well be proud. The buildings are commodious, well ventilated, and comfortable, while the ample grounds, which surround it, are laid out in artistic style.

Besides a large woolen factory, which manufactures some of the finest goods in the country, Chambersburg boasts a straw-board mill, a paper-mill, the Falling Spring furnace and steam flour mills, numerous planing, saw, and grist mills, and quite a number of other industries.

The Cumberland Valley Railroad shops and offices are at Chambersburg. The shops give employment to a considerable number of men. They were destroyed by the Confederates in 1864, but have been rebuilt in substantial and enlarged form.

The population of Chambersburg is about 6800.

MARION (STATION).

58 miles from Harrisburg ; 162 from Philadelphia.

THIS station takes its name from the little village near at hand, which was called after General Francis Marion, the "Swamp Fox of the Carolinas." The old town was settled as early as 1748, and was formerly known as "Smoketown." A new village is springing up at the station, which already rivals its parent in size.

SOUTH PENN JUNCTION.

59 miles from Harrisburg; 163 from Philadelphia.

THE Southern Pennsylvania Railroad, a branch, joins the main line here (mentioned elsewhere).

KAUFFMAN'S.

60 miles from Harrisburg; 164 from Philadelphia.

KAUFFMAN'S X ROADS, a flag station, is the point nearest the pic-nic grounds at "Brown's Mill," which, together with the ancient burying grounds of the Browns and their worthy line of ancestors and neighbors, lies in sight to the east of the road.

GREENCASTLE.

63 miles from Harrisburg; 167 from Philadelphia.

THIS town, called after a fishing station in county Donegal, province of Ulster, Ireland, was laid out by Col. John Allison in 1782. It is in the midst of a fertile and highly cultivated country, and possesses excellent school advantages. Its public buildings consist of a Town Hall, a large Public School, Presbyterian, Lutheran, Methodist, and German Reformed Churches. The inhabitants of this place and region around were exposed to the incursions of marauding Indians from 1755 to 1765. Near Greencastle, at the farm of Archibald Fleming in 1863, William Reels, the first Union soldier killed on Pennsylvania soil, fell in a skirmish with Confederate cavalry. The spot is in plain sight from the railroad just east of the town. Greencastle has about 1700 inhabitants.

STATE LINE (MASON AND DIXON).

68 miles from Harrisburg; 172 from Philadelphia.

AT this point the Cumberland Valley Railroad leaves Pennsylvania and crosses into Maryland, over the famous line which divides the North from the South. This line, known as Mason and Dixon's, was surveyed in 1767, by Charles Mason and Jeremiah Dixon, two English astronomers.

HAGERSTOWN.

74 miles from Harrisburg; 178 from Philadelphia.

PASSING Morgantown, a flag station, this the first town in Maryland is reached. The main line of the Cumberland Valley Railroad for many years terminated at.this place, which was formerly known as "Elizabethtown." Its history dates back to the far past. It is quite a railroad centre, the Cumberland Valley meeting here the Western Maryland Railroad, the Baltimore and Ohio, and the Shenandoah Valley. Hagerstown played no unimportant part in the late war. Its population is a little in excess of 6000.

DILLSBURG BRANCH, C. V. R. R.

THIS branch which extends from a point on the main line one mile from Mechanicsburg, a distance of eight miles to Dillsburg, in York county, its terminus, was constructed in 1873 for the purpose of opening up the inexhaustible mines of hematite ore in this section. In the vicinity of Dillsburg there are large deposits of magnetic and other valuable iron ore which are thus opened up to the market.

WILLIAMS' GROVE.

13 miles from Harrisburg; 117 from Philadelphia.

EVER since the opening of the Dillsburg branch, the picturesque country through which it passes has had considerable attraction for the people of the neighboring towns and cities. The grounds around Williams' Mill have been particularly popular. These grounds, generally known as

Williams' Grove, border on the banks of the Yellow
Breeches creek, and have a bountiful supply of delicious
water from a never-failing spring, while primeval trees
provide plentiful shade. The creek furnishes amusements
in the shape of boating and fishing, and the grounds are
spacious enough to admit of the enjoyment of various out-
door sports, the implements for which are usually on hand.
The level lawn and a commodious dancing-floor supply the
opportunity to those who desire to indulge in the art Terpsi-
chorean. A large kitchen and dining tent are erected on
the grounds, and a skilled caterer will be on hand to minis-
ter to the wants of the inner man, whenever his services are
required. This grove is known throughout Pennsylvania,
Maryland, and Virginia as the point where the tri-state picnic of the patrons of husbandry, known as the "Granger's
Picnic," is annually held. A feature of this picnic for the
ensuing year will be an exhibition of agricultural ma-
chinery, implements, and products. It will commence
Tuesday, August 30th, and close Saturday, September 3d.

DILLSBURG.

17 miles from Harrisburg; 121 from Philadelphia.

DILLSBURG, or Dillstown, as it was formerly called, is in
Carroll township, York county. It was incorporated April
9th, 1833. The various ore-banks in its vicinity make it a
busy place. It is the southern terminus of the branch of
the Cumberland Valley Railroad which leads to it.

SOUTH MOUNTAIN RAILROAD.

THIS railroad, which connects with the Cumberland Valley Railroad one mile east of Carlisle, was organized in
1868 for the purpose of utilizing more thoroughly the products of Pine Grove furnace and the South Mountain. The

line of the road extends through one of the wildest sections of the county, where nature has been lavish in the gift of beautiful scenery, rich deposits of ore, and springs of healing waters. Visitors to the Cumberland Valley should never fail to leave the main line at the South Mountain Junction, and take in the attractions of the Pine Grove region, descriptions of some of which follow.

MOUNT HOLLY SPRINGS.

24 miles from Harrisburg; 128 from Philadelphia.

THIS beautiful town has been long noted as one of the most healthful and delightful summer resorts in Pennsylvania, and bears the recommendation of eminent physicians as a place free from dampness, which is the general objection to mountain resorts. Hygrometric records of the atmosphere taken by Dr. B. F. Gibbs, Medical Inspector U. S. N., Washington, D. C., during the last fifteen days of August, 1880, from four daily observations, show for the locality a remarkably dry atmosphere as late as 11 P. M. Mount Holly is situated in a gap of the South mountain on the South Mountain Railroad, six miles from Carlisle, connections being made at South Mountain Junction with all through trains on the Cumberland Valley Railroad. Any one wishing a quiet and restful retreat during the summer will find this place very desirable for its beautiful scenery, cool, invigorating air, and pure spring water. Excursion tickets are sold from stations on the Pennsylvania Railroad, Northern Central Railway, and Baltimore and Potomac Railroad, as well as all along the line of the Cumberland Valley Railroad.

PINE GROVE PARK.

34 miles from Harrisburg; 138 from Philadelphia.

THIS popular picnic place has been for the past few years the favorite resort for excursionists from Harrisburg, Carlisle, and adjacent towns. It is delightfully situated in a romantic valley of the South mountains, the mountains rising directly in front of the Park, along the edge of which runs Mountain creek, adding very greatly to its beauty.

The Park was visited, during 1879, by 16,825 visitors, and in 1880 by 21,450.

FAMILY PICNIC.

Trains for the Park connect at South Mountain Junction with all the through trains on the Cumberland Valley Railroad. Leaving Harrisburg one rides through the Cumberland Valley eighteen miles to near Carlisle, and then directly across the valley, entering the mountain at Mt. Holly springs; thence up Mountain creek to the Park. Passengers are landed at their destination at once, not having to walk any distance.

The Park is a pine and oak grove, making a dense shade, and contains about thirty acres of ground. The mountains are well wooded and filled with numerous paths for those who desire to ramble, and enable them to be the discoverers of many pretty nooks and surprising views. The cleared ground or park proper is for the greater part level, with hills rising in the back ground. Here there is erected a pavilion sixty feet long and thirty feet wide, to be used either for assemblies or dancing; a public kitchen, at which excursionists on arrival find fires built and hot water ready, is near at hand, with ample table room, capable of seating six hundred persons. There is also a log cabin erected for ladies toilet rooms, in which will be provided all the necessary accessories of the toilet, and a lady attendant in charge. For the amusement of the children there are swings, croquet, and ball grounds, and a handsome set of flying horses, with elephants, deer, and chariots. The lake which is provided with boats covers about two acres and is not over two feet deep, making it perfectly safe for children. For the accommodation of ladies and gentlemen, there has been erected a building with two first-class ten-pin alleys. These numerous buildings will afford ample protection for all excursionists in case of rain. The water is supplied from three running fountains on the grounds, and is pure mountain spring water.

The management would especially call attention to the fact that no charge is made either for the grounds or for the use of the above buildings, flying horses, swings, boats, or bowling alleys.

For the accommodation of those not bringing provisions there has been erected a restaurant and dining room, with a seating capacity of one hundred and fifty; this will be in charge of Mr. B. S. Wilder, of the Mansion House.

Carlisle, Pa. All prices will be moderate. No intoxicating drinks of any character are allowed to be sold, and there is no place within six miles where liquor can be obtained. The management, owning all lands within at least three miles of the Park, can effectually prevent its sale or the annoyance of the visitors by outside parties.

MONT ALTO RAILROAD.

THIS road like the branches of the Cumberland Valley Railroad was built for the purpose of more perfectly utilizing the mineral wealth of the section of country through which it passes. It was opened in 1872, and extends from a point on the Cumberland Valley Railroad, three miles east of Chambersburg to Mont Alto Park and furnaces, a distance of a little over ten miles, with a branch road lately constructed to the town of Waynesboro, in the south-eastern section of the county. The scenery in the section through which this road passes surpasses any other in the valley, and Mont Alto and vicinity is now deservedly a most popular place of resort. The points along the road are as follows:—

FAYETTEVILLE.

55 miles from Harrisburg ; 159 from Philadelphia.

FAYETTEVILLE is the first station on the Mont Alto Railroad after leaving the junction, being also situated on the turnpike running from Chambersburg to Gettysburg. It is seven miles from the former, and eighteen miles from the latter place. During the invasion of Pennsylvania by the Southern army in July, 1863, this town lay within the line of the Confederate communication with Richmond ; the mails being carried through it. On one occasion a Southern mail was captured by some of the citizens of Fayetteville. This act of temerity, so incensed a force of Confederate cavalry near at hand, as to cause them to arrest a number of innocent citizens who experienced considerable difficulty in regaining their liberty. The place was formerly called " Milton Mills," but was changed to Fayetteville in honor of Marquis de LaFayette. The town contains five churches and two hotels. The population is between 600 and 700.

Mont Alto Park.

58 miles from Harrisburg ; 162 from Philadelphia.

Mont Alto is a post-office at the seat of Mont Alto Furnace and Park. The comfortable residence of Col. George B. Wiestling stands near the furnace buildings, and the homes of the miners and furnace men make quite a little village. The following description will give some idea of the beauties of Mont Alto Park, the famous summer retreat.

This delightful resort has been fitted up by Colonel George B. Wiestling, superintendent of the Mont Alto Railroad and Iron Works, and has become deservedly popular in the valley. Its beauties must be seen to be appreciated. The Park is about twelve miles from Chambersburg, Pa., and is reached by the Mont Alto Railway. The ride to the place is itself very fine, which is a great consideration to those who have a single day for recreation. It is not a pilgrimage through a desert to get water. Every step of the way may be enjoyed by those who have eyes to see the ever-varying glories of earth and sky. Beautiful as the Cumberland Valley is at any point, the most picturesque parts are to be seen only upon a near approach to the mountains, and unless the route between Mercersburg and Richmond can dispute the claim, the Mont Alto road stands unrivaled for the fine scenery it presents. One-half of the way is by the side of a sylvan stream of marvelous beauty, and almost all of the other half is in sight of white cliffs crested with dark rock pines that will remind a child of the places where the eagles build their nests, while all between the eye and the Blue Ridge outlined against the southern sky,

undulating fields and luxurious woodlands, make up a
scene that is simply enchanting. In passing through such
a section of country on one of our delightful summer days,
the common air seems charged with the life and inspiration
of eternity. No care-worn man, or health-broken woman,
or delicate child, can take the short journey without benefit.

To get a comprehensive view of the region through which
we pass, and indeed of the whole county of Franklin, one
should upon his arrival at Mont Alto, go to "Oak Knob,"
where Colonel Wiestling has built an observatory. It is six
hundred and forty feet above the Park, one thousand and four
feet above Chambersburg, and one thousand six hundred and
twenty feet above high tide of the Delaware river at Philadelphia. This point is less than seven hundred yards from
the fountain in the Park, and is accessible by a well marked
and not very difficult path. The view from this lookout is
really sublime. The Blue Ridge, twenty-five miles away,
sweeps around like a vast ampitheatre and bounds the horizon.
Green meadows, yellow, ripening grain, and pretty farm-
houses diversify the valley, and dot the mountain side.
The only drawback to this scene is that mind and heart
are oppressed by a sense of its *vastness*. An idea of this
may be gained by a comparison of particular objects in-
cluded in it, with the whole. When Alexander the Great
wished to build a monument for one of his generals, Staci-
crates proposed to carve Mt. Athos into an image so large
that a town might be built on one hand and a river flow
out of the other. The feat was too wild to be attempted
even by oriental extravagance. Had it been accomplished
it would have presented a spectacle different and more gro-
tesque, but not more grand and pleasing than some things
seen from these mountain tops ; and one is reminded of the
ambitious architect's design by noticing how man's work
is dwarfed by nature. From "Oak Knob," villages and
towns dwindle in the distance and look like mere specks in
the wide-spread landscape—toys that might be hidden in
the hand of Hephaestion. Chambersburg must be searched

for in the foliage, and large buildings look like white shells on a green bank. What floods of golden light are shed upon this vast expanse from time to time, those who have not seen the gorgeous sunsets of the region, can never imagine.

But while the view from "Oak Knob" is very extended, it is only by going to the "Narrows" that we get an idea of the grandeur of the mountain in detail. This name has been given to a pass made through the solid rocks by some convulsion of nature in past ages—showing a mighty upheaval before which the beholder stands after centuries long agone in awe and wonder. The pieces of rock are of fabulous proportions, and no one can estimate the force by which they were riven and strewn in wild confusion—there to lie in speechless testimony of that Almighty Power, which can smile at the lapse of time and the decay of empires.

The wealth of verdure around these rocks is almost as wonderful as the rocks themselves. Dark pines and hemlocks, with ferns of tropical growth, deepen into cypress shades, or light up in the glimmering rays of the sun. At one place thin-branched larches spread their boughs like a web of gossamer before the trees of deeper hue, and produce an effect that is wild and weird in the extreme. The rare beauties of this place have been partially exposed to view, and it promises to become as notable as any one scene at far-famed Watkins; and what greater beauties there are in the deeper depths no one yet knows. For the fissure in the rocks forms a romantic glen, through which foaming water leaps and tumbles over moss-covered stones all the way down the ravine to the principal grounds Col. Wiestling has prepared for his town-sick guests. A path has been opened all along this laughing brook up to the "Narrows," and the walk is so easy and so full of pleasing interest that a delicate lady will traverse it without weariness.

But apart from this, the park and pleasure grounds at Mont Alto exceed anything we know of in the State. The

"Park" proper is fitted up with all the appliances of a gymnasium. And what is more pleasing still, there are delightful rambles by limpid streams to numerous springs, with rustic bridges and seats at every desirable point, so that no one need be weary or thirsty.

The springs are almost without number. The Indian Spring, with its legend of the red man's adventures, and its more recent interest as being near the spot where Cook, one of John Brown's men, was arrested; the Twin Springs, the Cold Spring, the Pearl of Park, whose water is as cold as ice, and whose name well describes its character, and many others that can not be named, all contribute to the wonderful beauty of the place, and to the comfort of the visitor.

It is easy to see that the grounds at Mont Alto may be enlarged indefinitely. Already they are made up of so many charming little walks and sequestered spots, each hidden from the other, that no one can form an estimate of their extent. But with hundreds of people there at the same time, families and small companies may go off and find separate retreat, so no one need be annoyed by a crowd. This is what helps to make the place so desirable. It is now noted for the crowds of excursionists it draws from one end of the valley to the other.

If from what we have written any one should go there expecting to find splendid mason-work, in the way of walls, terraces and pavements built of marble; or to see statues of gods and heroes peeping out from among exotic plants, he will be disappointed, but he will find many rural comforts and beauties such as city people would gladly attain to if they only could. After all, this is the place where the fabled nymphs and naiads loved to dwell, and if the "scream of the locomotive" has scared them away, pretty girls and dear little children will people their favorite haunts and more than supply their places.

QUINCY.

THIS post town is situated in Quincy township on the road leading to Fayetteville. It is a German settlement, most likely an offshoot from York county. The township in which it is situated was settled as early as 1737.

NUNNERY.

A COMMUNITY of German Seventh-day Baptists with their own peculiar religion and code of morals, the last lingering relic in Pennsylvania of the old society of *Ephrata*, which flourished in this State about the middle of the eighteenth century. The curiously inclined should pay this community a visit.

WAYNESBORO.

THIS town which was formerly called "Wallacetown" after its founder John Wallace, and subsequently Waynesburg or Waynesboro in honor of General Wayne, the "Mad Anthony" of Revolutionary renown, is picturesquely situated at the base of the South mountain in the midst of a region of country of great fertility. The land upon which the town stands was taken up from the Proprietaries in 1749. The first house was erected by Michael McCoskrey. The town is noted for its manufacturing establishments, chief among which are the Geiser Manufacturing Company, builders of agricultural machines; Liedy & Co., lumber manufacturers; Frick & Co., steam engine and boiler works. The last-mentioned firm has just completed handsome and commodious buildings for the further accommodation of its business. There are eight churches and two hotels in the town. Its population is about 2000. Near Waynesboro is a remarkable cave, known as Needy's cave. Through it a subterranean stream courses its way. The interior of the cave is beautifully ornamented with innumerable crystal formations which sparkle profusely in the light of torch or candle. Under several streets of the town also are a number of caves, access to which is had from the cellars of dwelling houses.

— ◆◆◆ —

SOUTH PENN BRANCH.

THIS branch intersects the main line at a point seven miles south of Chambersburg, This road was originally built in 1870 by the "Southern Pennsylvania Railroad and Iron Company," for the purpose of transporting more readily the products of the old Mount Pleasant furnace, the most ancient enterprise of the sort in the county, to market. It extends right into the heart of the Blue mountains to its terminus at Richmond, touching Mercersburg with a branch. The country through which it passes rivals the Mount Alto section in beauty. A description of the principal places along the line follows:—

MERCERSBURG.

73 miles from Harrisburg; 177 from Philadelphia.

THIS place originally called "Smith's Settlement" but subsequently Mercersburg, in honor of Gen. Hugh Mercer, was a very important point in early provincial times; the nucleus of a settlement in the year 1730. Being a trading point with the Indians it was not an uncommon thing to see from fifty to one hundred pack horses there at one time loaded with merchandise, salt, iron and other commodities. The town now contains seven churches and two hotels. It was formerly the seat of Marshall College, which some years ago was removed to Lancaster and consolidated with Franklin College. Mercersburg College took its place, but that institution also closed its doors last year. During the late war the Confederates paid hostile visits to Mercersburg in the forays of 1862, '63 and '64. The population of the town is 1500.

37

LOUDON.

75 miles from Harrisburg; 179 from Philadelphia.

ONE of the most beautifully situated towns in the valley, Loudon lies at the base and in the shadow of the mountain, watered with its clear streams and healthful with its cool breezes. It is a very old place. Near it stood one of the line of forts erected during the French and Indian war—old Fort Loudon—which played a part of no mean importance in the event transpiring between the years 1755 and 1776. It has three churches and one hotel, with a population of about 400. This is the native place of the late Thomas A. Scott.

RICHMOND.

78 miles from Harrisburg; 182 from Philadelphia.

THIS is a little village of about 70 inhabitants, formerly known as the Mount Pleasant Iron Works, but now called Richmond in honor of Richmond L. Jones, the first president of the Southern Pennsylvania Railroad. A pure atmosphere and beautiful scenery mark the point.

STONE BRIDGE, WILLIAMSON, ROCKDALE, and LEHMASTER'S are flag stations between Chambersburg and Mercersburg. DICKEY'S, TROUT RUN and RYDER'S between Mercersburg and Loudon.

MARTINSBURG AND POTOMAC EXTENSION.

IN the year 1873, the main line of the Cumberland Valley Railroad was extended to Martinsburg, West Virginia; the new portion of the road being called the "Martinsburg and Potomac Extension." This line was important as being the connecting link between the Pennsylvania, the Cumberland Valley, and the Baltimore and Ohio Railroads.

FALLING WATERS.

PASSING WASHINGTON and WILLIAMSPORT stations, the little village of Falling Waters is reached. It is a post hamlet in Berkley county, West Virginia, on the Potomac river. The town has some importance in an historical point of view, being the scene of an engagement between portions of the Northern and Southern armies in 1863.

BEDINGTON.

88 miles from Harrisburg; 192 from Philadelphia.

THIS little village is six miles from Martinsburg, and is noted principally for the beautiful springs in its vicinity.

BERKLEY is a flag station between Bedington and Martinsburg, four miles from the latter place.

MARTINSBURG.

94 miles from Harrisburg; 198 from Philadelphia.

MARTINSBURG is an old-fashioned Virginia town. The land upon which it stands was taken up by Adam Stephens, and the town laid out in 1778, and derives its name from Col. T. B. Martin. Near it are traces of the road cut by Braddock's army on its fatal march westward. In its vicinity, also, within a few miles of each other, lived three officers of the Revolution—Alexander Stephens, Horatio Gates, and Charles Lee. The will of the last mentioned still remains of record in the clerk's office at Martinsburg. The town contains eleven churches, three banks, two female seminaries, four carriage factories, foundry, distillery, and planing mill, and other business interests. The population of the place is about 6000.

SHENANDOAH VALLEY RAILROAD
AND THE
WONDERFUL CAVERNS OF LURAY.

THE Shenandoah Valley Railroad which now connects with the Cumberland Valley Railroad at Hagerstown, Md., runs in a south-west direction, and entering the far-famed Shenandoah valley, has its present terminus at Waynesboro. Points of interest present themselves upon every hand along its line, brief descriptions of a few of which are here given :—

Five miles south of Hagerstown is the College of St James conducted under the auspices of the P. E. Church of the Diocese of Maryland, the main building of which was the old manor house of Gen. Sam Ringgold.

Close by is the famous battle field of Antietam, the road running through that portion of the field which was occupied by the left wing of the Confederate forces commanded by " Stonewall " Jackson, where the hardest fighting occurred.

In near proximity is Sharpsburg, with the " National Cemetery of Federal Dead," where rest the remains of 15,000 Northern soldiers, who fell on the bloody field of Antietam.

Crossing the Potomac river opposite Shepherdstown, about one mile down the river, the Potomac mills can be seen where two days after the battle of Antietam, " Stonewall " Jackson and Fitz-John Porter's corps had an encounter on the cliffs. A few miles below the mills is the ford where General Lee crossed his army after the battle of Antietam, and subsequently where he marched it northward for the invasion of Pennsylvania.

Shepherdstown, on the right bank of the Potomac river, is the oldest town in West Virginia, having been settled in 1734.

In the vicinity are numerous springs, one of which has long been known for its curative qualities.

It was here that the first successful trial was made in steam navigation. Here it was that James Ramsey publicly demonstrated, on December 6th, 1786, that a boat could be propelled by steam against the current of the river at the rate of four miles per hour. General Washington was one of his passengers.

Leaving Shepherdstown we pass by the ruins of two historic houses—"Bradford," the residence of the late Edmund I. Lee, a grandson of Richard Henry Lee, of Revolutionary fame, and "Fountain Rock," the former home of Alexander R. Boteler, a great-grandson of Charles Wilson Peale, the patriot artist of the Revolution.

The next point of interest is Charlestown, the county-seat of Jefferson. It is noted as the place where John Brown was tried and executed. It is named from the Christian name of its first proprietor, Colonel Charles Washington, a brother of the General. The ruins of "Harewood," the residence of Samuel Washington, another brother of the General, are one of the points of interest. Braddock's army passed through the place, and a well dug by the men is still in existence. In the neighborhood is the ruin of an old Episcopal church, built in the reign of George the Second; also a cave, where tradition has it Washington and others of the Masonic fraternity held their meetings.

Clarke county, of which Berryville is the county-seat, is full of historic houses. Here, for instance, is "Greenway Court," where for more than thirty years lived Thomas Lord Fairfax, Baron of Cameron, colonial proprietor of that princely domain of more than five thousand acres between the Rappahannock and Potomac rivers.

Not far from the old chapel is "Saratoga," the residence which General Daniel Morgan built for himself, compelling the Hessian prisoners he had captured at the surrender of Burgoyne to assist in its erection.

Between Luray and Shenandoah Iron Works is the celebrated Massanutton spring where thousands of people go annually to test its curative powers.

There is also another spring in the neighborhood which is visited by those troubled with malarial diseases.

The well-known Weyer's Cave, near Port Republic, is within three hundred yards of the Shenandoah Valley Railroad, and is a source of attraction to visitors to the Sulphur springs of Virginia, on the line of the Chesapeake and Ohio Railway.

At Luray and within half a mile of the Shenandoah Valley Railroad are the recently discovered but already celebrated caverns of Luray, which have been described as follows in brief.

LURAY CAVE.

THIS wonderful curiosity was discovered not by chance, but as the result of a long search, by Mr. B. P. Stebbins, formerly of Easton, Md., and some friends, who thought it likely, from surface indications, that there were caves in the neighborhood, and set to work to find them. They did a great deal of fruitless digging, and were duly ridiculed; but in 1878 they were rewarded by finding an entrance to what is claimed to be "the most beautiful cave in the world."

The tract of land beneath which it lies was bought by the discoverers of the cave, but is now the property of the railroad company, and considerable money has been expended in fitting it up with walks, stairways, &c., for the use of visitors. The entrance is from a small house, where visitors rest before and after entering the cave. The party is led by the guide down what might be the cellar stairs, only that in this case they descend probably forty feet, and are lined with massive masonry to support the roof at the entrance.

Passing under a low natural archway, the entrance hall is reached, a great cavern, beautifully decorated by

THE CATHEDRAL.

nature with weird stalactites, stalagmites, and other formations. Arrangements are about completed for lighting the cave with electric lamps, and of supplying the guides with magnesium lamps.

From the entrance hall, which seems to the visitor the perfection of cave scenery, various passage-ways lead to other apartments, chasms, and great halls, as much superior in size and grandeur to the entrance as that surpasses anticipations. No pen can describe the wonders of this cavern, which is probably two or three miles in length of its passage-ways, and descends in the ball room to a depth of two hundred and sixty feet from the surface.

It is in a limestone region, of course, and the stalactites and stalagmites formed by the crystallization of lime and magnesia, carried down to it in the water that drips from the roof, seem to meet here all the conditions necessary to their perfect development in an infinite variety of form. There is not merely the ordinary stalactite like an icicle, and its companion stalagimite built upward from the floor, but some of these have grown in the Luray cave to enormous size. There are cave crystals and cave pearls, stone cascades formed by the trickling of the lime-bearing water over inclined planes, horizontal stone growths, and branches or twigs and *blankets* made by the flattening out of stalactites and stalagmites. These are frequently recurved and present much of the appearance of a folded blanket suspended from the roof. The newly-formed stalactites are pure white; the older growths are colored in various shades by the iron or other minerals they contain. Some of the blankets mentioned above are very curious in this respect. While they are being formed the iron will be carried down to them for a time; then nothing but lime and magnesia; then more iron or some other mineral, the result being that the blanket will be given a border regularly striped in colors. When lights are placed behind the transparent stalactites the effect is very beautiful, the iron showing bands of red or reddish brown in contrast with the milk-white lime.

At every turning new creations of nature's fancy meet the eye, and a lively imagination can transform these queer formations into sculptured images of all kinds, and so we have a succession of more or less suggestive names given to them by visitors.

THE FISH MARKET.

Luray contains many beautiful springs, lined with crystals and filled to the brim with water so transparent that its presence is only made apparent to the eye by light reflected from its surface. The atmosphere of the cave appears to be entirely pure, and, though somewhat damp, the visitor who has thick shoes can wander about in every part without inconvenience. A good deal of money has been expended in fitting up walks and stairways and in digging out passage ways, so as to give head room. The main apartments can all be reached while walking upright or simply stooping under a fallen column, but there are vast caverns yet unexplored, to which the adventurous tourist can only go on hands and knees. Although smaller than the Mammoth Cave, Luray is pronounced by men who have seen both more interesting and beautiful."

THE VIRGIN FONT.

No extended description of the different points of interest in this cavern can here be attempted, and no description that can be written will give to the uninitiated anything like a true conception of this wonderful work of nature. It must be seen to be appreciated. Among the objects of interest are the Grand Entrance, Washington's Pillar, Stebbins' Avenue, Flower Garden, Amphitheatre, Muddy Lake,

Natural Bridge, Fish Market, Pluto's Chasm, Proserpine's Pillar, Crystal Spring, Skeleton Gorge, Imperial Spring, Brand's Cascade, Oberon's Grotto, Titania's Veil, Cinderella, Scale Column, Fallen Column, Saracen's Tent, Frozen Fountain, Diana's Bath, Angel's Wing, Cathedral and Organ, Tower of Babel, Entrance to Giant's Hall, Indian Squaw, Sultana Column, Giant's Hall, Double Column, Ball Room, Empress Column, the Lost Blanket, Campbell's Hall, the Sentinel and Spectre, the Vegetable Garden, Elfin Ramble, Mirror Lake, the Balcony, Crystal Spring, Snow Bank, Throne Room, Chanticleer, Tomb of the Martyrs, Idol and Cascade Springs, Chapman's Lake, Twin Lakes, The Lady of the Lake, the Ladies' Toilet Stand, Comet Column, Eagle's Wing, the Riding Whip, Cemetery, Bird's Nest, Bridal Chamber, Wet Blanket, Virgin Font, Grand Gulch, Katie's Secret, the Chimes, and the Mermaid.

From the foregoing description in brief of the rural retreats, summer resorts, picnic parks and pleasure places of the beautiful Cumberland Valley, a general idea may be derived of the unprecedented advantages offered by the Cumberland Valley Railroad to excursionists and those desiring a brief residence in the country during the summer. Every advantage of rapid transit in comfortable cars by frequent trains, with cheap rates (represented in excursion, weekly, monthly, and round-trip tickets), is offered by the Railroad Company, whilst the healthy climate and beautiful scenery of the country, the culture, social and religious privileges of the towns, and their unrivaled hotel facilities, render the Valley pre-eminent in its attractions. This is evidenced by the fact that scarcely a day during the summer passes without its picnic or excursion parties to one or the other, or all of the noted places of resort in this section.

SCHEDULE OF RATES AND TRAINS, HOTEL ACCOMMODATIONS, ETC.

RATES OF FARE.

The regular rate of local fare between stations on the Cumberland Valley Railroad is 3 cents per mile.

The usual form of mileage and commutation tickets good for individuals, families, and firms, are sold at Harrisburg and all principal stations, at greatly reduced rates.

Monthly tickets good for 54 trips during a calendar month between Harrisburg and the stations named below, will be sold during the summer at the following rates, viz:—

Harrisburg to White Hill, .	$3 00
" " Shiremanstown, .	4 00
" " Mechanicsburg,	5 00
" " Williams' Mill,	7 00
" " Dillsburg, .	8 00
" " Kingston, .	6 35
" " Middlesex, .	7 25
" " Carlisle, . .	8 00

For information in regard to special rates for excursion parties, &c., apply to A. H. McCulloh, General Ticket Agent, Chambersburg, James Clark, General Agent, Harrisburg, or to the ticket agents at the different stations.

THROUGH TIME-TABLE.
Cumberland Valley Railroad and Connecting Lines.

SOUTHWARD.

Leave NEW YORK, P. R. R	8.25 p m		4.25 a.m.	8.55 a.m.	3.15 p.m.
" PHILADELPHIA, P. R. R	11.55 "		9.00 "	12.10 p.m.	5.30 "
Arrive HARRISBURG, "	4.00 a.m.		12.01 p.m.	3.45 "	8.40 "
Leave PITTSBURG, P. R. R	8.25 p.m.		4.20 a.m.	8.25 a.m.	7.20 a.m.
" ALTOONA, "	12.30 a.m.		8.25 "	11.55 "	2.35 p.m.
Arrive HARRISBURG, "	3.55 "		12.01 p.m.	3.15 p.m.	7.30 "
Leave HARRISBURG, C. V. R. R	4.15 a.m.	7.15 a.m.	12.30 p.m.	4.10 p.m.	8.45 p.m.
Arrive CARLISLE	5.04 "	8.10 "	1.25 "	5.05 "	9.40 "
" CHAMBERSBURG	6.15 "	9.25 "	2.40 "	6.23 "	10.55 "
" HAGERSTOWN	7.10 "	10.30 "	3.36 "	7.30 "	
" MARTINSBURG		11.50 "	5.15 "	8.40 "	
Leave HAGERSTOWN, S. V. R. R	7.30 a m	11.00 a m	3.55 p.m.		
Arrive CHARLESTOWN, W. VA	8.28 "	11.51 "	5.03 "		
" LURAY, Va	10.45 "	1.45 p.m.	7.25 "		
" WAYNESBORO', VA	1.20 p.m	4 05 "	10.15 "		
" WHITE SULPHUR SPRINGS	6.50 "	8.00 "			

NORTHWARD.

Leave WHITE SULPHUR SPRINGS.	....	8.25 p.m.	....	6.00 a.m.	....
" WAYNESBORO, VA.	....	1.30 a.m.	....	10.55 "	8.30 p.m.
" LURAY, VA.	....	3.55 "	....	1.25 p.m.	6.15 "
" CHARLESTOWN, W. VA	....	6.24 "	....	3.30 "	8.47 "
Arrive HAGERSTOWN	....	7.30 "	....	4.30 "	10.00 "
Leave MARTINSBURG, W. VA	....	7.10 a.m.	10.15 a.m.	3.40 p.m.	....
" HAGERSTOWN, MD	....	8.00 "	12.10 p.m.	4.40 "	10.05 p.m.
" CHAMBERSBURG, PA	4.25 a.m	9.05 "	1.05 "	5.33 "	11.05 "
" CARLISLE	5.54 "	10.30 "	2.25 "	6.45 "	12.25 a.m.
Arrive HARRISBURG	6.45 "	11.30 "	3.20 "	7.40 "	1.21 "
Leave HARRISBURG, P. R. R	7.00 a.m.	12.20 p.m	3.35 p.m.	8.00 p.m	1.45 a.m.
Arrive PHILADELPHIA	10 10 "	3.20 "	6.35 "	11.35 "	5.15 "
" NEW YORK	1.05 p.m.	6.25 "	9.30 "	3.45 a.m.	7.55 "
Leave HARRISBURG	8.00 a.m	12.20 p.m	4.05 p.m.	10.25 p.m.	2.20 a.m.
Arrive ALTOONA	1.55 p.m.	4.00 "	8.00 "	2.25 a.m.	5.45 "
" PITTSBURG	8 50 "	7.30 "	12.01 a.m.	7.00 "	9.15 "

PULLMAN SLEEPING CARS run through between New York, Philadelphia, and White Sulphur Springs on the train leaving New York at 8.25 P. M., Philadelphia at 11.55 P. M., returning on the train leaving White Sulphur Springs at 9.00 P. M.

LOCAL TIME-TABLE.

Cumberland Valley Railroad and Branches,

IN EFFECT JUNE 7th, 1881.

UP TRAINS.—Harrisburg to Martinsburg.

STATIONS.	Miles	N. Y. Express	Accom. Train	Mail Train	Philad'a Express	Carlisle Accom.	Har'g Express
		A. M.	A. M.	P. M.	P. M.	P. M.	P. M.
Leave HARRISBURG	0	4.15	7.15	12.30	4.10	6.15	8.45
" BRIDGEPORT	1		7.25	12.40	4.20	6.24	8.55
" WHITE HILL	3		7.30	12.44	4.25	6.28	9.00
" SHIREMANSTOWN	5		7.35	12 50	4.31	6.34	9.05
" MECHANICSBURG	8	4.40	7.44	12.59	4 39	6.42	9.14
" KINGSTON	12		7.53	1.08	4.48	6.51	9.23
" MIDDLESEX	14		7.58	1.13	4.53	6.57	9.28
" SOUTH MT. JUNCT	18		8.05	1.20	5.00	7.05	9.35
" CARLISLE	19	5.04	8.10	1 25	5.05	7 10	9 40
" GREASON	24		8.21	1.39	5.17		9.53
" KERRSVILLE	25		8.25	1 43	5.21		9.56
" NEWVILLE	30	5.27	8.35	1.53	5.31		10.06
" OAKVILLE	31		8.43	2.02	5.40		10.15
" SHIPPENSBURG	41	5.51	8.57	2.16	5.57		10.30
" SCOTLAND	47		9.10	2.29	6.10		10.44
" MONT ALTO JUNCT	48		9 15		6.15		
Arrive CHAMBERSBURG	52	6.15	9.25	2.40	6.23		10.55
Leave CHAMBERSBURG	52	6.18	9.30	2.45	6.30		
" MARION	58	6.31	9.45	2.58	6.45		
" GREENCASTLE	63	6.43	10.00	3.10	7.00		
" STATE LINE	68	6.56	10.15	3.23	7.13		
Arrive HAGERSTOWN	74	7.10	10 30	3.36	7.30		
Leave HAGERSTOWN	74		11.03	3.40	7.55		
" WILLIAMSPORT STAT'N	81		11.19	4.15	8.10		
" FALLING WATERS	85		11.30	4.35	8.21		
" BEDINGTON	88		11.36	4.48	8.27		
Arrive MARTINSBURG	94		11.50	5.15	8.40		
		A. M.	A. M.	P. M.	P. M.	P. M.	P. M.

☞ Through Coach on New York Express from Harrisburg to Waynesboro', Va., and on Mail Train from Philadelphia to Waynesboro', Va.

DOWN TRAINS.—Martinsburg to Harrisburg.

STATIONS.	Miles.	Har'g Express	Carlisle Accom.	Mail Train.	Phil'a Express	N. Y. Express	Night Express
		A. M.	A. M.	A. M.	A. M.	P. M.	P. M.
Leave MARTINSBURG	1			7.10	10.15	3.40	
" BEDINGTON	6			7.24	10.40	3.54	
" FALLING WATERS	9			7.30	10.52	4.00	
" WILLIAMSPORT STAT'N.	13			7.40	11.19	4.15	
Arrive HAGERSTOWN	20			7.55	11.55	4.32	
Leave HAGERSTOWN	20			8.00	12.10	4.40	10.05
" STATE LINE	26			8.17	12.25	5.54	10.20
" GREENCASTLE	31			8.32	12.38	5.06	10.33
" MARION	36			8.45	12.50	5.18	10.45
Arrive CHAMBERSBURG	42			9.00	1.02	5.30	11.00
Leave CHAMBERSBURG	42	4.35		9.05	1.05	5.33	11.05
" MONT ALTO JUNCT	46			9.15		5.40	
" SCOTLAND	47	4.46		9.19	1.15	5.44	11.16
" SHIPPENSBURG	53	5.00		9.35	1.29	5.57	11.30
" OAKVILLE	59	5.15		9.50	1.43	6.11	11.45
" NEWVILLE	64	5.27		10.00	1.55	6.20	11.55
" KERRSVILLE	69	5.37		10.10	2.05	6.30	12.05
" GREASON	70	5.41		10.14	2.09	6.34	12.09
" CARLISLE	75	5.54	8.00	10.30	2.25	6.45	12.25
" SOUTH MT. JUNCT	76	5.59	8.05	10.35	2.30	6.50	12.30
" MIDDLESEX	80	6.06	8.12	10.43	2.37	6.57	12.37
" KINGSTON	82	6.11	8.17	10.49	2.42	7.02	12.42
" MECHANICSBURG	86	6.20	8.26	11.00	2.51	7.10	12.51
" SHIREMANSTOWN	89	6.27	8.34	11.09	3.00	7.19	1.00
" WHITE HILL	91	6.32	8.40	11.15	3.05	7.25	1.05
" BRIDGEPORT	93	6.36	8.45	11.20	3.10	7.30	1.10
Arrive HARRISBURG	94	6.45	8.55	11.30	3.20	7.40	1.20
		A. M.	A. M.	A. M.	P. M.	P. M.	A. M.

☞ Through Coach on Harrisburg Express from Chambersburg to Philadelphia, and on Mail Train from Waynesboro', Va., to Philadelphia. Also, on New York Express from Waynesboro', Va., to Philadelphia.

C. V. R. R.—DILLSBURG BRANCH.

Mail Train.	Accom. Train.	Miles.	STATIONS.	Miles.	Accom Train.	Mail Train.
P. M.	A. M.	Lv.	Arr.		A. M.	A. M.
4.10	7.15	0	HARRISBURG	17	6.45	11.30
4.31	8.15	8	MECHANICSBURG	9	6.15	10.50
	8.23	9	DILLSBURG JUNC	8		
5.05	8.45	13	WILLIAMS' GROVE	4	5.45	10.15
5.10	8.50	14	H. & P. JUNCTION	3	5.40	10.12
5.25	9.00	17	DILLSBURG	0	5.30	10.00
P. M.	A. M.		Arr.	Lv.	A. M.	A. M.

C. V. R. R.—SOUTH PENN BRANCH.

Mixed Train.	Mail Train.	Miles.	STATIONS.	Miles.	Mail Train.	Mixed Train.
A. M.	P. M.	Lv.	Arr.		A. M.	P. M.
4.15	12.30	0	HARRISBURG	78	11.30	7.40
8.00	5.00	52	CHAMBERSBURG	26	9.00	5.30
8.45	5.20	58	MARION	20	8.35	5.18
8.00	4.40		HAGERSTOWN		8.00	7.30
8.32	5.06		GREENCASTLE		8.32	5.06
9.20	5.41	65	Arr. WILLIAMSON Lv.	13	8.13	4 33
9.35	5.50	69	LEHMASTER'S	9	8.03	4.13
10.00	6.00	73	MERCERSBURG	10	7.50	3.50
10.50	6.22	75	LOUDON	3	7.28	3.05
11.05	6.30	78	Arr. RICHMOND Lv.	0	7.20	2.50
A. M.	P. M.				A. M.	P. M.

SOUTH MOUNTAIN RAILROAD.

No. 6 Mixed.	No. 4 Pass.	No. 2 Pass.	STATIONS.		No. 1 Mixed.	No. 3 Pass.	No. 5 Pass.
P. M.	P. M.	A. M.	LV.	Arr.	A. M.	P. M.	P. M.
4.10	12.30	7.15	............HARRISBURG,.........		11.30	3.20	7.40
5.00	1.30	8.05	........SOUTH MOUNTAIN JUNC........		10.30	1.20	6.50
5.50	1.56	8.31	..........MOUNT HOLLY SPRINGS........		9.45	12.50	6.25
6.50	2.30	9.00	..........PINE GROVE PARK...........		8.30	12.10	5.50
P. M.	P. M.	A. M.	Arr.	Lv.	A. M.	P. M.	P. M.

MONT ALTO RAILROAD.

No. 4 Mail.	No. 2 Accom.	STATIONS.		No. 1 Mail.	No. 3 Accom.
P. M.	A. M.	LV.	Arr.	A. M.	P. M.
4.10	7.15	................HARRISBURG...........		11.30	7.40
6.30	9.05	................CHAMBERSBURG...........		9.25	5.48
6.30	9.18	..........MONT ALTO JUNCTION...........		9.10	5.35
7.10	9.50	..........MONT ALTO PARK...........		8.40	5.00
7.45	10.30	..........WAYNESBORO'...........		8.00	4.25
P. M.	A. M.	Arr.	Lv.	A. M.	P. M.

Special Trains will be run for large Excursion Parties to Mont Alto Park.

HOTEL ACCOMMODATIONS, &c.

At Mechanicsburg.

MERCHANTS' HOTEL, located on Main street, can accommodate fifty persons, rates from $3.50 to $6.00 per week. David Kimmel, proprietor.

MURRAY HOUSE, located on Railroad avenue, can accommodate fifteen persons, rates from $3.50 to $6.00 per week. James Murray, proprietor.

NATIONAL HOTEL, located on West Main street, can accommodate fifteen persons, rates from $3.50 to $6.00 per week. John McClure, proprietor.

AMERICAN HOUSE, located on Market street, can accommodate twenty persons, rates $3.50 to $6.00 per week.

MRS. LINDSAY'S PRIVATE BOARDING-HOUSE, can accommodate fifteen persons, rates $3.50 to $5.00 per week. Located on Locust street.

At Mt. Holly Springs.

CENTRAL HOTEL, on Balto. avenue, J. H. Williamson, proprietor, can accommodate sixty at from $7 to $8 per week. Children half price. Five minutes' walk from South Mountain Railroad depot.

MULLEN HOUSE, on Balto. avenue, near depot of South Mountain Railroad, Isaac Mengel, proprietor, can accommodate one hundred and fifty, at rates from $30 to $35 per month. Children and servants, $20.

UNITED STATES HOTEL, D. Z. Geyer, proprietor, can accommodate fifty; rate, $5 to $8 per week. Situated on Balto. avenue, four minutes' walk from South Mountain Railroad depot.

MT. HOLLY HOUSE, situated on Balto. avenue, can accommodate four or five; rate, $7 per week; G. D. Gensler, proprietor; ten minutes' walk from the depot.

Mrs. Charles Mullen, on Balto. avenue, three minutes' walk from depot; can accommodate six or eight persons. House pleasant, terms reasonable. (Apply by letter.)

Milton Saylor, postmaster, has pretty cottage, two doors above post-office, for rent; terms, $8 per month; seven rooms.

Philip Harman has pretty house on Balto. avenue for rent. For terms, &c., apply to P. Harman, Mt. Holly Springs.

At Carlisle.

FLORENCE HOTEL, Main street, between Hanover and Bedford streets. Five minutes' walk from depot. Can accommodate fifty. $8 to $12 per week. Gas, water, and bath.

MANSION HOUSE, corner Pitt and Main streets. All trains stop at door. Can accommodate seventy-five. $7 to $12 per week. Gas, water, and bath.

GARBER HOUSE, corner Main and Bedford streets. Can accommodate twenty. $3.50 to $5 per week. No bar. Seven minutes' walk from depot.

LEREW HOUSE, corner Hanover and Walnut streets. Can accommodate sixty. $3.50 to $5 per week. Eight minutes' walk from depot.

FARMERS' AND DROVERS', corner Hanover and South streets. Seven minutes' walk from depot. Can accommodate twenty-five. $4.50 to $5 per week.

AMERICAN HOUSE, Hanover street, between Main and Louther streets. Can accommodate twenty-five. $4 to $5 per week. Five minutes' walk from depot.

FRANKLIN HOUSE, corner Public Square and Hanover street. Can accommodate fifteen. $5 to $8 per week. Three minutes' walk from depot.

Boarding-Houses.—Miss Barbara Egolf, No. 7 North Hanover street. Can accommodate thirty. $6 to $8 per week. Transient boarders, $1 to $1.50 per day.

Mrs. A. K. Stewart, Louther, near West street. Can accommodate three. $5 per week. Transient boarders, $1 per day.

Mrs. Shafer, No. 10 South Hanover street. Can accommodate five table boarders.

Houses to Let.—Three houses, eight rooms each, North Bedford street, seven minutes' walk from depot. Inquire of D. Sipe, No. 16 North Hanover street.

One house, seven rooms, gas, and water, south-east corner Pitt and North streets. Inquire on premises.

One house, eight rooms, north-west corner Pitt and North streets. Inquire of J. O. Fridley, Hanover street.

At Shippensburg.

SHERMAN HOUSE, Corner of Main and Railroad streets, can accommodate thirty-four, rate $5 per week. I. A. Quigley, proprietor.

MANSION HOUSE, South Railroad street, can accommodate twenty, rate $5 per week. H. Stumbaugh, proprietor.

CENTRAL HOTEL, South Railroad street, J. E. Hughes, proprietor. Rate, $4 per week.

At Chambersburg.

WASHINGTON HOUSE, accommodation for seventy-five; three minutes' walk from depot. $5 to $10 per week.

MONTGOMERY HOUSE, accommodation for seventy-five; five minutes' walk from depot. $5 to $10 per week.

NATIONAL, five minutes' walk from depot; accommodation for thirty. $6 to $10 per week.

FRANKLIN HOUSE, seven minutes' walk from depot; accommodations for twenty-five. $4 to $8 per week.

INDIAN QUEEN, ten minutes' walk from depot; accommodations for twenty. $4 to $6 per week.

At Greencastle.

FRANKLIN HOUSE, located on Carlisle street, near Cumberland Valley Railroad depot, can accommodate thirty. Rate, $4 to $6 per week. James Shirley, proprietor.

NATIONAL HOTEL, located on the public square, can accommodate twenty-five. Rate, $4 to $6 per week. E. Brosius, proprietor.

At Hagerstown.

BALDWIN HOUSE, situated on Washington street. Rate, $7 to $14 per week.

NEWCOMER HOUSE; rate, $7 per week, or $25 per month.

FRANKLIN HOUSE; rate, $8 per week.

MANSION HOUSE; rate, $5 to $7 per week.

www.ingramcontent.com/pod-product-compliance
Lightning Source LLC
Chambersburg PA
CBHW031802090426
42739CB00008B/1128